Archaeology and Ancient Cultures

UNCOVERING THE CULTURE OF
ANCIENT MESOPOTAMIA

By Alix Wood

PowerKiDS
press
NEW YORK

Published in 2016 by
The Rosen Publishing Group, Inc.
29 East 21st Street, New York, NY 10010

Cataloging-in-Publication Data

Wood, Alix.
Uncovering the culture of ancient Mesopotamia / by Alix Wood.
p. cm. — (Archaeology and ancient cultures)
Includes index.
ISBN 978-1-5081-4663-6 (pbk.)
ISBN 978-1-5081-4664-3 (6-pack)
ISBN 978-1-5081-4665-0 (library binding)
1. Iraq — Civilization — To 634 — Juvenile literature. I. Wood, Alix. II. Title.
DS71.W66 2016
935—d23

Editor: Eloise Macgregor
Designer: Alix Wood
Consultant: Rupert Matthews

Photo Credits: Cover, 1, 20 bottom, 21 top, 22 bottom © Dollar Photo Club; 2 © Howard Smith; 4 top © National Museum of Iraq; 5 top © Arlan Zwegers; 5 bottom © M. J. Artesanos; 6 bottom © Kunsthistorisches Museum, Vienna; 7 top © Ur Region Archaeology Project; 7 bottom, 8 top, 9 bottom, 10 bottom, 11 top, 14, 15 bottom, 16 top, 18, 19 middle, 21 bottom, 23 top © Trustees of the British Museum; 8 bottom © Kiengi Ki Uri; 12 top © The Pergamon Museum, Berlin; 13 bottom © www.army.mil; 15 top © Brooklyn Museum; 16 main © Major Mike Feeney; 17 top © Josep Renalias; 17 bottom © Louvre Museum; 19 top © Agatha Christie 20 top © Behnam Farid; 22 top © National Library of Israel/Schwadron Collection; 23 bottom © The Israel Museum; 25 top © Yale Art Museum; 25 bottom © Gill Gillerman/Yale; 26, 27 bottom © Julie Blacksher; 28 top © Classical Numismatic Group; 28 bottom © 101st Airborne Division; 29 top © Staff Sgt. JoAnn Makinano; 29 bottom © Multi-National Corps, Iraq Public Affairs; all other images are in the public domain

Manufactured in the United States of America

CPSIA Compliance Information: Batch #: BW16PK For Further Information contact Rosen Publishing, New York, New York at 1-800-237-9932

CONTENTS

MESOPOTAMIA

Mesopotamia is the name for the area around the Tigris and Euphrates rivers. Mesopotamia literally means "land between two rivers." In Greek, "meso" means "middle" and "potamia" means "river." In modern times the area is now Iraq, Kuwait, northeast Syria, southeast Turkey, and southwest Iran.

Mesopotamia is often called the "Cradle of **Civilization**" as some of the earliest great civilizations began there. In the Bronze Age the Sumerian, Akkadian, Babylonian, and Assyrian empires all began in what is now Iraq.

This copper head of an Akkadian king is over 4,200 years old!

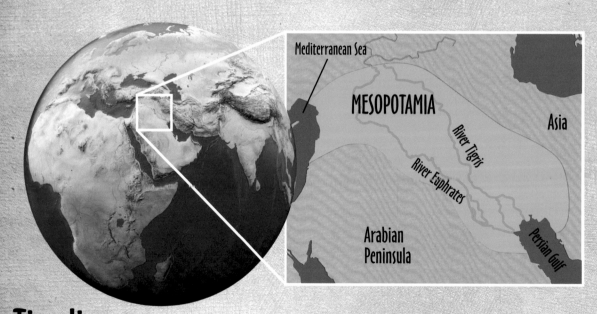

Mediterranean Sea

MESOPOTAMIA

Asia

River Tigris

River Euphrates

Arabian Peninsula

Persian Gulf

Timeline
A colored band by the page number shows each site's time period

5000-c 2400 BCE	c 2400 - 2100 BCE	c1900 - 609 BCE	c650 - 539 BCE
Sumerian Empire	Akkadian Empire	Assyrian Empire	Babylonian Empire

The ruins of Dura-Europos on the Euphrates River

The Sumerians of Mesopotamia formed the first ever civilization! They invented writing and government. The Akkadians followed and formed the first empire, joining the Sumer city-states under one ruler. The Akkadian language became the main language for most of the history of Mesopotamia. The Babylonians, from the powerful city of Babylon, created vast empires in the area. They were the first to write down laws. The Assyrians were warriors and ruled much of the Middle East at different times. In later times, invading armies of Persians, Greeks, and Romans put an end to the rule of the Assyrians and the Babylonians.

Artifact Facts

Is this the world's first battery? In 1938 German **archaeologist** Wilhelm Konig unearthed a small clay jar, a copper cylinder, and an iron rod. The Baghdad Battery is believed to be about 2,000 years old. If filled with vinegar, the jar produces about 1.1 volts of power! This photograph is of a reconstruction.

c539 - 330 BCE	c330 - 247 BCE	c247BCE -224 CE
Persian Empire	Greek Seleucid Era	Parthian Era

THE FIRST CITY

Eridu

An old photo of a dig at Eridu

The Sumer people are believed to have made the first ever city at Eridu. It was built around 5000 BCE, when **nomads** began to form villages in the area between the Tigris and the Euphrates rivers. Gradually the villages grew into cities. Eridu was one of a group of cities in the area often called the "Cradle of Civilization."

Eridu is best known for its temples, called **ziggurats**. A ziggurat looks like a stepped pyramid with a flat top. Each city had its own god which was worshiped at the temple. Priests would perform rituals or sacrifices there.

Artifact Facts

Some historians think that the large ziggurat at Eridu might be the Tower of Babel. In a Bible story, while people were building a tall tower, God made them speak different languages so they couldn't understand each other! This painting of the Tower of Babel is by Pieter Bruegel the Elder.

When a team of Iraqi archaeologists explored Eridu in the 1940s, they found amazing temples dating back to **prehistoric** times! Eridu was near the sea and by a river, but also close to a hot desert. To water their crops the people built canals. They made mud-brick buildings and reed huts to live in. The amazing temple complex was built of mud brick, with a small pit dug around it that may have been filled with water. Eighteen older mud-brick temples were found underneath the unfinished large ziggurat! People moved out of Eridu when moving sand dunes and rising salt water made the place difficult to live in or grow crops.

Sumerian craftsmen were skilled in stonework, metalwork, and pottery. Beads found in Sumer graves were usually made of gold, **lapis lazuli**, **carnelian**, and silver. In this necklace, four cones of coiled gold wire attached to a gold disc form the central pendant.

Sumerian pottery was very fine. The inside of this bowl, found at the nearby town of Susa, was painted using oil from the cedar tree.

7

A ROYAL CEMETERY

The great city of Ur was first occupied around 4,000 BCE. Excavations in 1922 led by Sir Leonard Woolley revealed an amazing Sumerian royal cemetery. Woolley found many treasures. One day Woolley even reported "We are doing marvelously well: I'm sick to death of getting out gold headdresses!"

This beautiful game board was found at the royal cemetery. Two players race their pieces around the board. Players can only start after certain numbers are thrown on the dice. The rosette spaces are lucky spaces. We know how to play because a set of rules was found in Babylon by archaeologists.

rosette space

The Royal Game of Ur is about 4,500 years old!

The ziggurat at Ur.

Archaeologists found 1,850 burials, 16 of which were thought to be royal tombs. In one of the tombs, Woolley found a beautiful box, known as the Standard of Ur (below). One tomb, thought to Queen Puabi's, had many sacrificed people buried with her. The discoveries made headline news, and the site attracted many visitors. One of these visitors was the famous crime author, Agatha Christie. She went on to marry one of Woolley's archaeologists, Max Mallowan, and set one of her murder mystery novels, "Murder in Mesopotamia" at the dig at Ur.

Agatha Christie

Artifact Facts

This box, known as the Standard of Ur, was found in the cemetery next to a skeleton of a sacrificed man. It has beautiful mosaic scenes of war and peace on each side. On the war side, a Sumerian army charges and captures prisoners. The peace side shows men bringing food to a banquet, while a singer and musician entertain.

peace side

war side

NINEVEH TABLETS

Nineveh, on the eastern bank of the Tigris River, was one of the oldest and greatest cities of Mesopotamia. The city was surrounded by a massive stone and mud-brick wall. Stone towers and fifteen monumental gateways were built into the wall. People at the gateways checked people entering and leaving the city. They were probably barracks and weapon stores, too.

Archaeologist Austen Henry Layard's favorite childhood story was "The Arabian Nights." He wanted to travel to the place the story was set. His dream came true when he **excavated** the great cities of Nineveh and Nimrud. He found amazing artifacts, such as the carved hunting scene below left. He discovered enormous statues with men's heads and winged bulls' bodies guarding the gates, and many tablets with a strange language carved on them.

Austen Henry Layard

Cuneiform is one of the earliest types of writing. King Ashurbanipal had a library of thousands of cuneiform tablets at his palace at Nineveh. Some of the tablets contained the legend of Gilgamesh, ruler of Uruk, and his search for ever-lasting life (left). As cuneiform wasn't used after around 200 CE, no one knew how to read any of the tablets at first!

This is the 11th of 12 tablets, where Gilgamesh is warned of a flood and builds a boat to keep people and animals safe.

To work out how to read cuneiform, archaeologists needed to find text that was repeated in another known language. Carved high on a cliff, along the road between Babylon to Ecbatana, archaeologists found what they needed! The Behistun Inscription was in three different scripts. Darius I of Persia had the inscription made. The Old Persian version, and a list of Persian kings, helped experts crack the code!

Artifact Facts

In 1835, a British army officer, Henry Rawlinson, climbed the cliff and copied the inscriptions. He translated them when he found the same list of kings in a Greek text by Herodotus. He returned in 1843 to copy other, harder to reach, sections, with the help of a brave local boy, some ropes, and some planks!

ASSYRIAN ASHUR

Ashur

Ashur, on the western bank of the river Tigris was the first capital of the powerful Assyrian Empire, which ruled its own state in Mesopotamia from 1250 BCE to 612 BCE. The city was an important center, as it lay on a trade route that ran through Mesopotamia. Ashur was well-protected, surrounded by the river, a double wall and a big moat.

Despite this, in 612 BCE Ashur was destroyed, along with other great Assyrian cities such as Nineveh. They were attacked by a joint army of Babylonians, Medes, and Persians. The city was partially re-built and lived in until the 1300s but was never as wealthy as before.

Artifact Facts

Ashur had several temples, including one to Ishtar, the Sumerian goddess of love and war. This **incense** burner was found at the Ishtar Temple. Burning incense was an important part of some ceremonies.

the Tigris River

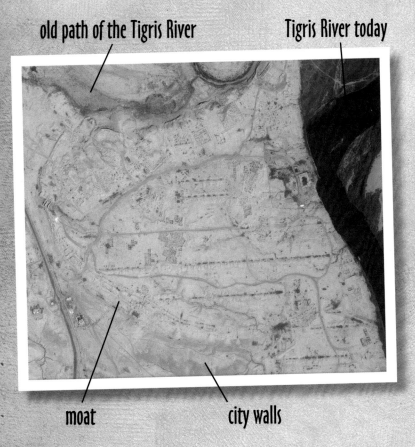

old path of the Tigris River

Tigris River today

moat

city walls

Using satellite images of Earth, archaeologists can often see features of a site that they easily can't see from the ground. In this image of Ashur you can clearly see the ruined walls. You can also see that the Tigris River used to flow to the north of the city. This explains why the city walls did not go all around the north edge.

Archaeology can be at risk from natural events such as earthquakes, or when a country is at war. Many sites in Mesopotamia have been damaged either by accident, or deliberately. Deliberate damage of monuments has happened throughout history. Ashur is also at risk from a proposed river dam that might flood part of the site.

US soldiers provide security at the Gate of Tabira, Ashur, during a **UNESCO** visit to the site.

NIMRUD

Nimrud was a major Assyrian city, and was Assyria's capital when King Ashurnasirpal II was on the throne. Archaeologist Austen Henry Layard explored the site between 1845-51. Layard discovered several pairs of colossal figures guarding the palace entrances. Known as **lamassu**, the statues have a man's head, the body of a lion or bull, and wings. Layard shipped two of the enormous lamassu to the British Museum in London by barge. Later, museums at Paris, Chicago and New York had lamassu shipped to them, also.

Artifact Facts

When Layard discovered the lamassu he wrote in his diary "I shall not myself easily forget this enormous head appearing from the earth, at the bottom of a deep trench, like some giant arising." Somehow, he managed to ship the huge pair of lamassu to the British Museum in London by barge!

Layard found some fine stone panels decorating the walls of the palace of Ashurnasirpal II. The panels showed scenes from the king's life. The panel below probably shows an incident when Ashurnasirpal's army was marching along the Euphrates River to the enemy capital, Suru. Three enemy men, in long robes, were forced into the river to save themselves. Two are blowing into inflated animal skins to help keep themselves afloat. Ashurnasirpal's archers are on the left, shooting at the enemy.

The remains of some cuneiform script. Layard cut off the bottom to make the panel easier to transport!

The Nimrud site was abandoned for many years, but Max Mallowan thought Nimrud had more left to discover. He was right. Mallowan found thousands of **ivory** carvings. His wife, Agatha Christie, helped clean the finds. She had an unusual method—she often used a fine knitting needle and her face cream! She said this helped get dirt out of the tiny holes without harming the ivory.

An ivory carving that Mallowan found at the bottom of a well, showing a lioness eating a man.

15

ANCIENT BABYLON

When the Sumer civilization began to lose power, the Babylonian civilization grew. It was named after its most famous city, Babylon. The city was surrounded by huge walls and a **moat**. At its center was an enormous ziggurat. Outside the city walls, a network of canals watered the fields. The city was famous for its spectacular hanging gardens.

Babylon

Archaeologists have been able to find out a great deal about Babylon. Old texts describe the city in detail. Babylon was crowded, as everyone lived inside the city walls. The narrow streets had tall houses on each side. People threw their trash into the streets. Every so often, workers would cover the trash with a layer of clay, raising the level of the streets!

An artist's impression of the Hanging Gardens of Babylon

The remains of the city of Babylon, now in modern-day Iraq.

The Ishtar Gate was one of eight gates in the city walls. It was decorated with bulls and dragons made from glazed brick. A wide, paved road with its walls decorated with lions and dragons, led to the temple and tower.

A bull from the Ishtar Gate

No one was sure if the Hanging Gardens of Babylon really existed. Nebuchadnezzar II was said to have built the gardens as a present for his homesick wife. They were considered one of the wonders of the ancient world. In the early 1900s, German archaeologist Robert Koldewey thought he had discovered the legendary garden's foundations under one of the grand palaces.

Koldewey discovered a basement with stone arch ceilings. Ancient texts said that only two places in the city were made of stone, the north wall, and the hanging gardens! As the north wall had already been found, Koldewey believed he had found the cellar of the gardens. Modern archaeologists believe the arched rooms were stores, though, as carved lists of supplies were later found in the ruins.

Artifact Facts

King Hammurabi of Babylon had the city's laws written onto clay tablets and etched into stone for all to see. This stone, shaped like a giant finger, has the Code of Hammurabi written around the base. Some of the laws were very strict, for example if a son hit his father, his hands were cut off!

THE EYE TEMPLE

Tell Brak

I n 1925, Frenchman Antoine Poidebard was flying over the Syrian desert. He saw that something was creating shadows on the ground under the evening sun. He realized what he was seeing were man-made structures. Eleven years later, Max Mallowan went to excavate the spot.

Tell Brak is one of the largest and most important archaeological sites in Mesopotamia. The word "tell" means a mound, created by human occupation. The large mound at Tell Brak was made over many centuries. Most Mesopotamian buildings were built using mud bricks. Over time the bricks crumbled and walls needed to be rebuilt. Gradually the city was raised higher by building on top of earlier structures.

Artifact Facts

Mallowan found an extraordinary temple at Tell Brak known as the Eye Temple. It was filled with thousands of small figures with large eyes. They date from around 3,300 BCE. These eye **idols** may have been offerings to the gods.

Eye idols like this one have only been found at Tell Brak. Eye designs have been found on objects from the cemetery at Ur and in some temples.

Mallowan's wife, author Agatha Christie, took photographs of the dig. Here, workers are raising baskets of artifacts from the underground rooms of the Eye Temple using a winch.

Because temples sometimes had valuable goods buried there, they were targets for robbers. In one robbers' tunnel, Mallowan discovered this small stone head. The head probably once had beautiful jewelry on it, which the robbers had stolen. A vertical groove at the back of the head with nail holes on the sides suggest the statue was originally attached to a pole. This head is one of the earliest human sculptures ever found.

The remains of one of Tell Brak's palaces

PERSEPOLIS

Persepolis

Persepolis was once the capital of the Persian Empire. The name Persepolis is Greek for "city of Persians." The city was full of magnificent buildings. The Persian king, Darius I, wanted to build an impressive center for his Empire. His son Xerxes, and grandson Artaxerxes I completed the fine city. It became one of the richest cities in the world, with many gold and silver treasures.

Disappointingly, archaeologist Ernst Herzfeld, left, found hardly any treasure in 1931 when they came to excavate the site. Why? The city had been **looted** and burned by Alexander the Great in 330 BCE. Plutarch, an ancient Greek historian and writer, wrote that Alexander had used 20,000 mules and 5,000 camels to carry all the treasure away! Persepolis lay in ruins.

Buildings are just as exciting as treasure for archaeologists. Ernst Herzfeld uncovered this beautiful decorated stairway.

The most impressive buildings at Persepolis include decorated stairways and gateways, the kings' palaces, a vast meeting hall with 100 stone columns, the treasury, the stables, and the chariot house. The largest number of finds were from the royal storehouse in the treasury. Archaeologists found hundreds of clay tablets with cuneiform inscriptions. After the fire the clay in the tablets, that may otherwise have crumbled, was fired and in great condition. The writing on the tablets gave archaeologists a lot of information about life in Persepolis.

Artifact Facts

Alexander and his army did a very thorough job of looting. Archaeologists did find these small arrowheads in the Treasury, along with some horse's bridle ornaments and sword scabbard tips.

DEAD SEA SCROLLS

● The Dead Sea

In spring, 1947, a local goat-herder and his cousin were searching the cliffs for a lost goat, when they found a cave. They threw a stone into the cave to try and scare the goat out. All they heard was the sound of breaking pottery. Puzzled, they entered the cave, and found several jars. Inside some old cloth wrappings were ancient scrolls.

When Israeli archaeologist Eliezer Lipa Sukenik heard about the scrolls' discovery, he traveled to meet a dealer who had bought four of the scrolls. In a secret meeting at the Jerusalem border, the dealer held up a fragment of leather for the professor to examine through the wire fence. Sukenik immediately recognized the ancient writing.

Sukenik examining the scrolls

the Qumran caves

The scrolls contained ancient religious writings, important to both Christian and Jewish people. As word spread, archaeologists, and Bedouin treasure hunters, raced to find more scrolls.

Ten other caves were found, containing around 850 scrolls! In 1952, in Cave 3 archaeologists found two mysterious copper scrolls, listing what may be sites of buried treasure hidden in the area!

Not all the finds were scrolls. In 1962 at another search site at Wadi Daliyeh, a cave was discovered that held the skeletons of 205 people. Ancient papers found with the bodies identified them as wealthy Samaritans who fled after the invasion of Alexander the Great in 333 BCE. They were probably killed by Alexander's troops.

One of the broken jars found in the cave where the first Dead Sea Scrolls were discovered.

Artifact Facts

This fragment is from the Temple Scroll, found in the 11th cave at Qumran. Most of the scrolls are written in Hebrew like this one, but some are in Aramaic. The scrolls were probably the library of a Jewish **sect**, who hid them when the Roman army advanced against them.

DURA-EUROPOS

Dura-Europos

The city of Dura-Europos was first Greek, then Parthian, and finally Roman. It was bordered on the east by the Euphrates River, and to the north and south by steep valleys. On the west side a huge wall was built to protect the city. The city was originally called Europos. It later became known as Dura, meaning fortress.

Dura-Europos is quite unique. After the city was abandoned in 256–7 CE nothing was built over it, so the archaeology was not destroyed. The city stood at the crossroads of two major trade routes, one going from East to West and the other along the Euphrates River. This meant that Dura-Europos was home to a mixture of cultures.

The Palmyra Gate entrance to the city probably led along a trade route to the wealthy city of Palmyra.

In 1920, a British soldier digging a trench in the area uncovered some colorful wall-paintings. Archaeologists began to explore the site. They uncovered a temple, and then war stopped the dig.

At a later dig, Roman arms and armor were found in near-perfect condition. How were they so well-preserved? During a **siege**, the Romans found their enemy had been tunneling under the city walls. To stop them, they filled a street of buildings with rubble! The Christian chapel, Jewish synagogue, and many other buildings were buried and protected. Archaeologists found tunnels on both sides of the city walls. They also found the skeletons of soldiers trapped inside the tunnels. Coins found in the tunnels date the siege to 256 CE.

Artifact Facts
This Roman shield was found flattened and in several pieces, but still in remarkable condition.

This frieze (right) was found in the Jewish synagogue. Experts think the scenes from the Bible were used to educate people about its stories. This wall painting shows the battle of Eben Ezer.

THE PILATE STONE

Caesarea Maritima was built on the Mediterranean coast by Herod the Great about 25–13 BCE. If you have read any Bible stories you may recognize his name, as he was the king who was jealous of Jesus in the nativity story. Herod named the city after the Roman Emperor, Augustus Caesar. Archaeologists in the 1950s and 1960s found remains from other periods, but most of the buildings were Roman.

Around the city, a strong wall and a wide moat protected the harbor to the south and east. There was a temple **dedicated** to Caesar, and a stadium for chariot and horse races. A theater in south of the city faced the sea, with thousands of seats. and a semi-circular marble floor.

Caesarea Maritima

Artifact Facts

At the theater, archaeologists found a damaged limestone block with an inscription. The reason this was so exciting is because it is the only stone ever found with an inscription mentioning the name "Pontius Pilatus." In Bible stories, Pontius Pilate was the Roman who sentenced Jesus to death.

"U" is written "V" in Roman script

TIVS·PILATVS

the Roman aqueduct

Herod built an **aqueduct** to bring fresh water into the city. An extra channel was added when the city needed more water. The aqueduct was an amazing feat of engineering. The spring water had to be brought from the mountains. The angle of the channels had to be right so the water would flow. In some portions, the aqueduct was supported by rows of arches.

Herod's grand palace was built on a rocky area jutting into the sea. The palace building had a beautifully decorated swimming pool in the center, surrounded by columns.

Today, much of the city is underwater because of an earthquake, and so Caesarea Maritima has opened the world's first underwater museum! Divers are given waterproof maps and can visit an underwater quay, tower, piers, brickwork, Roman jars, and anchors!

Herod's swimming pool was filled with fresh water from the aqueduct.

PARTHIAN HATRA

Hatra

H atra was founded in around 200 BCE by the Seleucid Empire. It was captured by the Parthians from modern-day Iran. It became an important center for religion and trade. Hatra held against repeated attacks by the Roman Emperors Trajan and Septimius Severus. The city was protected by its high, thick walls and over 160 towers. It is said the Parthians bombarded attackers with jars filled with scorpions!

A coin of Shapur I

The city became the capital of the new Arab Kingdom of Araba, a part of Parthian Empire, which was governed by Arabian princes. The city eventually fell to the Sassanid Empire in 241 CE and was destroyed. A legend says that Nadira, a daughter of the Arab ruler, betrayed the city to the Sassanian king, Shapur I. Shapur killed her father and married Nadira, but later had her killed too!

The ruins of Hatra. Many of the temples are built in a Roman style.

When Austen Henry Layard visited the site in 1846 he could not accurately date the city, because of the curious mix of building styles and temple gods. The city's buildings were a mix of all sorts, including Greek, Mesopotamian, and Arabian styles. There were temples to gods from many different cultures and religions.

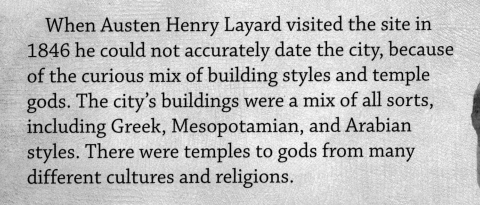

Artifact Facts

Often known as the Lady of Hatra, this statue is thought to be of the goddess Shahiro. She is made in typical Parthian style with her eyes staring straight ahead into space. She stands outside the Temple of Shamash, the Mesopotamian spirit of the Sun. The statue is thought to have been destroyed in 2015 by Islamic State militants.

The Temple of Mrn at Hatra is built in a typical Greek style.
The columns and decorative friezes are similar to temples all over Greece.

frieze

columns

GLOSSARY

aqueduct An artificial channel for carrying water.

archaeologist A scientist that studies past human life, fossils, monuments and tools left by ancient peoples.

carnelian A hard tough reddish quartz used as a gem.

civilization An advanced stage of social development.

cuneiform Made up of or written with marks or letters shaped like wedges.

dedicated To nominate something in someone's honor.

excavated Removed earth from an area, usually by archaeologists searching for finds.

idols An image worshiped as a god.

incense Material used to produce a fragrant odor when burned.

ivory The hard creamy-white substance of which the tusks of a tusked mammal (as an elephant or walrus) are formed.

lamassu An Assyrian protective deity, often shown as having a human's head, a body of a bull or a lion, and bird's wings.

lapis lazuli A deep blue gemstone.

looted To rob, especially openly and by force.

moat A deep wide trench around the walls of a castle or fortress that is usually filled with water.

nomads A member of a people that has no fixed home but wanders from place to place.

prehistoric Of, relating to, or existing in times before written history.

sect A religious group having beliefs that differ greatly from those of the main body.

siege The placing of an army around a fortified place or city to force it to surrender.

UNESCO United Nations Educational, Scientific, and Cultural Organization.

ziggurats A rectangular stepped tower, sometimes surmounted by a temple.

FURTHER INFORMATION

Books

Doeden, Matt. *Tools and Treasures of Ancient Mesopotamia* (Searchlight Books - What Can We Learn from Early Civilizations?). Minneapolis, MN: Lerner Publications, 2014.

Feinstein, Stephen. *Discover Ancient Mesopotamia* (Discover Ancient Civilizations). Berkeley Heights, NJ: Enslow Publishers, 2014.

Samuels, Charlie. *Technology in Mesopotamia* (Technology in the Ancient World). New York, NY: Gareth Stevens Publishing, 2013.

Due to the changing nature of Internet links, PowerKids Press has developed an online list of websites related to the subject of this book. This site is updated regularly. Please use this link to access the list:

www.powerkidslinks.com/AAC/Meso

INDEX